JUST C-H-I-L-L-L

Stress Management Guide for Students

Brooks Harper

JUST C-H-I-L-L-L
Copyright © 2021
Brooks Harper Enterprises LLC

ISBN: 978-0-9853146-2-0
Library of Congress Control Number: 2021900122

Published by Brooks Harper Enterprises, LLC
Lexington, SC

Book Cover Design by KarrieRoss.com

For Information Contact:
Brooks Harper
brooksharperspeaks@gmail.com
www.brooksharper.com

JUST C-H-I-L-L-L
Student Stress Management Guide

Foreword

Stress is something that everyone struggles with, but some people can manage it better than others. I myself have struggled with how to manage it for years. My dad has always has been my #1 supporter who pushed to find ways to help me learn how to handle it. He has chosen to share these life principles with others by putting them in writing.

"Just C-H-I-L-L-L" is not just an easy read book that will help you learn to manage stress, but a guide to help you through every aspect and stage of your life. I have had the opportunity of being taught these skills for many years thanks to my dad. This book is designed to help guide you through the stressful times in your life.

Katelin Harper

Introduction

When my daughter, Katelin, was in the 7th grade it was reported that some of the students at her school had head lice. I remembered the same thing happening at my school when I was a student. The thought of it makes my head itch. We were instructed as parents to carefully inspect our child's hair, and our own, and treat it if there was any evidence of lice. No Biggie! Her mom looked through her hair that evening as we watched tv in the living room, and we were relieved to not find anything nesting in her head! However, her mom spotted something else in her head that gave us pause. There was a perfectly round bald spot the size of a nickel in the back of her scalp. It was so smooth it looked as if hair had never grown there.

After making sure she hadn't done anything like pull it out or shave it somehow, we made an appointment with her pediatrician. Her doctor inspected the bald spot and assured us it was a ring worm and gave us an anti-biotic to treat it. We were cautiously optimistic, but down deep we were not convinced it was a ringworm. After a few days of being on the medicine, not only was there no sign of hair growing back in the spot, but we began to notice new bald spots. Her hair was beginning to show up in the bathtub. We knew this was definitely not a ringworm. We made an appointment with a dermatologist. After a biopsy of a new spot right in the front top of her head (which we were pretty upset about the chosen location for the biopsy) it was confirmed she had alopecia areata. In case you've never heard of it I will give you a brief definition in my own words. Alopecia areata is an auto-immune disorder in which the body's white blood cells attack its hair follicles, causing hair to fall out.

We were somewhat relieved to know what the cause was, but upset to learn that there is really no cure. In our frustration and ignorance, I had the following conversation with the doctor:

Me: "How did she get alopecia?"

Doctor: "She didn't get alopecia; its genetic. She was born with it."

Me: "Well we haven't seen any evidence of this in the past 12 years, why is it just now showing up?"

Doctor: "Your daughter is probably stressed out!"

(Stress is a trigger for activating alopecia as well as many other auto-immune disorders and health problems such as lupus and thyroiditis. Stress and anxiety have also been linked to ulcers, dental problems, arthritis and stomach trouble.)

The thing that had me scratching my head was: What would a 12 year old, beautiful, outgoing girl be stressed out about?

Apparently a lot! I had forgotten how stressful this time in my life was. It doesn't matter if you are in elementary, middle, high school or college. School is stressful! Not to mention everything else you have going on in your life. Studying, deadlines, exams, papers, relationships, sports, activities and life in general. As these things all seem to be happening at once, you start to get stressed out, worried and increasingly anxious.

Then someone comes along and says, "Hey, you need to chill out!" I have two problems with that advice: (1) it is easier said than done, and (2) no one really tells us how to chill!

Come to find out, my daughter was mixing it up with older students who were giving her a hard time at school. She's the type that if you put her in the room with 30 students, 28 of the students can love her to pieces, but guess where she spends all of her time, energy and effort? You guessed it...mixing it up with the other 2! Instead of celebrating and enjoying the 28, she loses sleep and hair worrying about the 2 students, who probably didn't give her much thought at all. More on how to handle these 2 later on.

Katelin got the double whammy! Once we identified one of the main sources of stress in her life, she had a whole new source of stress....HER HAIR WAS FALLING OUT! It was like a downward spiral. The harder you try to stop stressing the more you stress. The larger the clumps of hair that fell out, the larger the hair pieces she had to wear. Until finally she was in a full wig, with no eyebrows or eye lashes!

Now here come her parents saying, "CHILL OUT! LET IT GO!" Realistically, the only thing she had let go of was her hair. If you have hair on your head, be thankful for every individual hair, because sometimes we don't appreciate what we have until it is gone.

We all get stressed out sometimes! Some of us are stressed out all of the time! What is your stress and anxiety level right now on a scaled from 1 to 10?

>1-3 It's all good! (1-3 doesn't last long!)

>4-8 Getting amped up!

>9-10 Completely flustered!

I don't think anyone has the answer for completely eliminating stress from your life, but I do believe there are answers to learning how to deal with it in healthy, effective ways.

I am writing this book so you can learn how to JUST CHILL! C-H-I-L-L-L CHILLL. (When you say it, you have to hold the "L." C H I L L L. Say it with me: "C H I L L L." You are already chilling, and you don't even realize it! Now more than ever it is critical to learn how to identify the sources of stress, worry and anxiety, be aware of them and learn how to effectively cope so you can thrive.

It has been widely reported that this generation is the most anxious generation in human history. Everyone is all keyed up and wound extremely tight. It takes less and less to set people off into a frenzy! We need to learn to Just C-H-I-L-L-L.

C-H-I-L-L-L stands for:

C – Count your assets

H – Have Healthy Habits

I – Invest in yourself and the return in others

L – Let Loose

L – Lean on Others

L - Laugh

I will explain what each of these tools mean, why they are important and how to practically implement them into your life. The concepts are simple, but not necessarily easy. The cool thing is you have this book to help guide you through this stressful time and as a reference for years to come.

We are going to go through them one by one, a step at a time and suggest actions steps after each chapter. You may find that one particular step works particularly best for you. Another step may work better in a different situation. The awesome thing is you will have all 6 at your disposal to help manage your stress and anxiety. The key is to figure out the formula and balance that works best for you. Let's get started!

Chapter 1

Count Your Assets

When I first became a professional speaker, I was being considered for hire by a company that sent speakers into high schools to talk about student success. In order to become eligible to speak, you had to learn the 45 minute presentation by heart and fly to Cincinnati to deliver it in front of a panel of professional speaker trainers and receive certification. Giving a speech is hard enough, but giving a scripted speech to an audience who knows every word you're supposed to say is another story. After months of memorization and practice, I was in the airport at the gate set to fly out of Columbia, SC with my nose buried in the script. As this guy walked by me, I lifted my head out of the script, looked up and briefly noticed the entire side of his face had been burned. I quickly looked back down to not get caught staring. (When I see something so traumatic that has happened to someone, I often wonder how or what took place to cause this type of injury, but it's not like you can simply ask.) It so happened he was seated right behind me on the plane. I could hear him behind me having a conversation with the passenger next to him that seemed normal enough.

When we landed it Atlanta, I headed to my connecting flight to Cinci. The hallways in the Atlanta airport are so long, automatic treadmills have been installed to help speed you along and make the journey less taxing. These might be useful in school, right? They are actually pretty fun to walk on because it's like you're gliding along effortlessly. However, I was having this conversation with myself as I stepped onto the treadmill, "Brooks if you are going to be a bigtime speaker, you have to learn to let the treadmill do its job!" I decided to let the treadmill carry me to the end of the corridor.

The problem in the Atlanta airport is if you stop walking on the treadmill you might get run over by another traveler. I hugged the right side of the walkway and turned around to make sure I was in no one's way, and guess who is walking right toward me? You guessed it! The guy with the burns!

We made eye contact and I couldn't look away. I didn't want him to think that I didn't want to look at him….you know what I mean? He was burned bad! His ears were burned off, he didn't seem to have any lips, no eye lashes.

I also had that feeling like "me and this guy are definitely going to have a conversation", but I had no clue what I would say. (It stresses me when I don't know what to say!) It turns out I didn't have to say much. He walked right up to me and started this conversation:

Him: "How are you?"

Me: "OK, How are you?"

Him: "Fantastic! Where are you flying?"

Me: "Cincinnati. Where are you flying?"

Him: "San Francisco. Now why would you be flying to Cincinnati?"

Me: "I am going to be a professional speaker!"

Him: "Interesting! That's what I do, I speak all over the world!"

At this point it dawned on me what to say to him: "Wow, I bet you have a story to tell!" He said, "Yes I do!" We just didn't have time for him to tell it to me. I realized we had gotten to the end of the treadmill. The gate to his plane was in one direction and mine in the opposite direction. He said his name was Joel as he reached out to shake my hand and that's when I noticed he didn't have any hands! I had been so focused on him and our conversation that I didn't even see his hands were burned off. (It seems to me we should focus on who a person is and not what they look like, right?)

Question: How do you do shake a person's hand who doesn't have one?

Answer: Simple! You shake what they offer you!

I reached out and shook the little nub at the end of his wrist and told him how much I appreciated meeting him. I had been stressed, anxious and worried about learning the script for my upcoming presentation, and delivering it well enough for them to give me a shot, but as I walked toward the airplane I was having a new conversation with myself that went something like this:

"Brooks, you don't have problems! I mean, here's a guy who if he woke up this morning and was in a bad mood or having a bad day, you would give him some space. If he was negative or cynical, you would be somewhat understanding, seeing this guy has obviously had a rough go at it." But he wasn't like that at all. He was as positive as could be and the most enthusiastic person I had ever met. My perspective was changed forever. I was seeing through a new, more focused lens; the lens of gratitude. Sometimes that is all we need -- just a little adjustment in the lens by which we view our situation.

The training weekend went great! I knocked the presentation out of the park, and the company hired me as part of its speaking force, but I couldn't get this guy out of my mind. Meeting him was life changing. I searched his name online and learned he had a book about the story of his life. Of course, I bought the book and read it!

Often in life, much of what happens to us in a negative way may be things we bring upon ourselves by the choices that we make. On the other hand, sometimes in life things happen to us that are not of our making. Things just sometimes happen. That's Joel's story!

His book told about the inflamed car accident he and his family were in when he was only 22 months old. This accident would burn over 80% of his body, stretch the limits of the medical profession and force him to fight for every breath to save his life. It detailed the dozens of painful surgeries and how he would deal with his appearance and people staring at him the rest of his life! He didn't go to school the first day of first grade. Instead, they decided to bring all of the students from his school into the auditorium and show a home video of him. They were preparing his classmates for his arrival, because his physical appearance might be too shocking and difficult for other students to understand.   The school counselors explained that he, like them, was a student and just happened to be different, and that it was perfectly fine to be different! He showed up the 2nd day of classes and was the most popular student at the school! By senior year he was an awesome soccer player! Guess what you don't need in order to play soccer? HANDS!!!

I am reminded of this great quote. It is definitely in my top 5 quotes of all time:

"Did you hear about the man who was singing the blues because he had no shoes, until he met a man on the street who had no feet?"

Instead of sitting around thinking about all of the sports and other things that he couldn't do without hands, he focused on a sport that doesn't require the use of hands! How brilliant! How inspiring!

After meeting Joel and then reading his book, the lens by which I viewed my plight in life was permanently adjusted. Things came into crystal clear focus for me. The lens of gratitude turns "can'ts" into "cans" and dreams into plans by permitting us to see the possibilities instead of the obstacles.

Gratitude for what you have is one of the greatest cures for stress, worry and anxiety. Focusing on what you do have, instead of what you don't have, is an incredibly powerful stress reducer!

The science proves it! The University of California-Davis did a study which concluded that people who "practice gratitude" periodically throughout the day lowered the cortisol in their bodies by over 23%. Did you know that cortisol is the stress hormone in our bodies? When we get stressed out, our bodies produce increased levels of cortisol.

Focus on what you have instead of what you don't have!

Digital Harbor High School in Baltimore, Maryland has one of the finest track programs in the country, but guess what they do not have... A TRACK! How can a school have a track program when it doesn't even own a track? The coach decided they didn't need a track to have a track team. Instead he focuses on what they do have at the school, a 4th floor. Their school, like a lot of inner-city schools, goes straight up in the air instead of being spread out, due to the lack of available land. The coach has the team upstairs every day running drills and hurdling obstacles. They are so well conditioned, they show up to meets and blow other teams off their own tracks. In fact, they believe the lack of having a track motivates them to compete at an even higher level. It would have been so easy to decide not to even have a track program due to not having a track. No one would blame the school. Instead, they pushed past the limiting beliefs and barriers of excuses to achieve the improbable. They didn't say, "We can't because....They said, "We can because!" Do you see the difference in attitude? Do you see the difference in appreciation? Do see the difference perspective can make?

Not having a track makes their appreciation for winning even greater!

This is the power of gratitude! By appreciating what you have instead of regretting what you don't have, stumbling blocks become stepping stones! When these students go off to colleges that have more resources than their high school, they appreciate the new facilities that much more and often over achieve. Do I believe the students at Digital Harbor deserve a track now? Of course I do, and maybe one day they will! For now it's not their reality and it's not their excuse!

Joel didn't decide to not play sports because he didn't have any hands, rather he found a sport that doesn't require the use of hands. This gives him an even greater appreciation for his feet!

Can you think of areas in your life where you have limited your possibilities by focusing on obstacles and excuses instead of what is available? Have you been saying "I can't" instead of saying, "I can because?" The difference is the conversation and the thought process.

I often hear people accuse this generation of having an attitude of entitlement. Entitlement is a feeling like you are owed something. Have you heard this too? The problem with feeling like you're owed something or constantly believing you were slighted is it can lead to excusing yourself from doing and being your best.

Appreciation is the Kryptonite of Entitlement! Gratitude leads to an attitude that says, "No one owes me anything, because I have so much already!" Many people think that if they could just win the lottery all of their problems would be solved when in reality their problems would be multiplied. Money is a multiplier of what is already there. Documentaries have chronicled the families of lottery winners, and how unprepared they were to handle that much cash and how it ultimately destroyed them. There is an old saying, "You may have what you want, but you may lose what you have!"

It is quite unfortunate that we don't fully appreciate what we have until it's gone! Have you ever noticed that when you lose something or someone in your life you suddenly discover how much value it or the person had in your life? It is far better and healthier to be grateful for what we have while we have it than to regret not appreciating it once it is gone.

Count Your Assets

One of the first things we did after discovering Katelin's alopecia was have her write down everything she was thankful for on a large note card. She made a list of every possession, person and organization in her life for which she had an appreciation.

I call it an Asset List. It could also be called a Gratitude List, Thankful List or an Appreciation List. You can call it whatever you like. It is a list that inventories every person, place, thing or event in your life that is worthy of value and appreciation.

With a bit of encouragement and some examples to get her started, she compiled a rather long list of assets! She was thankful for her vision, hearing and sense of smell. She was thankful for her bedroom, bed, dresser and the clothes inside of it. Her mom and I even made the list at some point for which we were extremely thankful! When she found herself getting stressed or discouraged about her hair loss, she would pull out her thankful list and focus on those things that were in her possession and in her life. Reminding yourself early and often is a great tool in your tool belt for stress management. If you make a daily habit of counting your assets proactively, you'll find it of tremendous benefit to your overall attitude in all of your ventures and endeavors. It may be you don't get invited to a party or event, don't sweat it. Instead, be grateful for all of the other cool events you do participate in. If you don't get a particular present you were expecting, be excited and grateful for the presents you do get.

Take a moment and count your assets. Make a list of everything you appreciate and are grateful for. Get a sheet of paper, index cards, journal or type them in your notes on your phone. Don't be shy with the ink! It can be a person you're thankful for or even a trip you got to go on. It doesn't matter. If you are thankful for it, then write it down.

Carry your list with you.

Take a moment periodically throughout your day and review your list. Especially when you find yourself getting stressed and anxious. Reminding yourself of those valuable assets in your life has a tremendous calming effect. It helps us chill out and bring back into perspective the things that are most important. Sometimes the source of trouble can actually be the loss of one of the items on your asset list. Loss is a fact of life and happens to all of us. This is why it is important to have a nice, long asset list for appreciation diversification. In the event of a loss, a healthy asset list reminds us that it's not a total loss. Though we grieve for a period of time, we are encouraged and comforted by the value and gratitude that does remain.

One of the people most important to me in my childhood was my grandmother, Nana. Nana helped my mom make sure we had the things we needed after my dad split on us when I was nine years old. She helped my mom get an affordable car so she didn't have to take the city bus to work. She made sure there were presents for birthdays and holidays. Sadly, she passed away during finals week of my last semester in college. I was taking 6 classes (18 credit hours), trying to get across the finish line. It was an extremely stressful time, and her death could not have been worse timing. But that's how it goes sometimes. Things seem to stack up right on top of us. I was fortunate to have many assets in my life to reach out to and draw upon, not to mention a treasure chest of invaluable memories with her. When you make your list of assets, be sure to really put thought into it. You are going to find out how loaded you are.

I also encourage you not to wait until you are stressed to use it; be proactive and go over it every day. Consistently counting your assets will improve your overall happiness and provide great stress relief when times are really tough.

Reminders and Action Items from Chapter 1

1) Adjust your gratitude lens to the things you do have.

2) List some obstacles in your life that you feel may be preventing you from achieving your goals. What are some actionable steps you can take as an alternative?

3) Count Your Assets. Make a list of every person, possession or event that holds value for you and you appreciate.

4) Keep your Asset List handy and review it periodically throughout your day.

Chapter 2

Have Healthy Outlets

Do you know when you are experiencing stress and anxiety? Can you identify when stress and anxiety are present? Everyone is managing their stress and anxiety in some form or fashion whether they realize it or not. I have a good friend who was battling anxiety and depression; he had no idea he was anxious or even depressed until he ended up pretty sick. To manage stress and anxiety effectively, it is essential to be aware that they are present and have a plan to deal with them. Being unaware and/or unprepared leads to poor management and perhaps unhealthy habits.

I know of a recent high school graduate who went off to college in a highly competitive engineering program. He was as academically prepared as any student could be, but not really mentally and emotionally ready for the stress and pressures that come with advancing to the next level. When the stress that often comes with freshman year like, course load, financial obligations, social pressures, etc. set in, he turned to the meal plan to cope with it. Unfortunately, he gained 40 pounds his first semester. Without realizing it, he was stress eating to manage it all.

This is only one example of how easily we can develop poor outlets for "dealing" with stress and anxiety. I also know of a middle school student who plucked out every single one of his eyebrows before realizing they were gone! Can you imagine looking in the mirror to shockingly discover your eyebrows disappeared only to realize it was you who plucked them out? It sounds unimaginable, but things like this happen more often than you might think. This is why I focus on HEALTHY outlets. We all experience stress and we are all vulnerable to developing unhealthy outlets for coping with it as well. You can start to see that there is a difference between managing stress and "dealing" or "coping" with stress. One is healthy, and the others are unhealthy. Can you think of ways you may currently be dealing with stress and anxiety in an unhealthy way?

Awareness is the key to managing stress and anxiety in a healthy manner. You must first be aware that stress and anxiety exist in your life and equally aware of how you are responding. Here are some healthy outlet suggestions for managing stress and anxiety. This is not meant to be a comprehensive list, but some ideas you might try or at least get you on the right track to developing your own.

Personal Hygiene

Taking care of your personal hygiene makes you feel better. I always feel great after a haircut. Even our dog Cooper is the same way. When his hair starts to get so long that it grows out of the corner of his eyes impairing his vision (when it gets like this the little fella has to turn his head sideways to see), we ask him if he's ready for a haircut and a bath. He goes absolutely bonkers, wagging his tail, jumping up on us in an emphatic "yes!" The funny thing is watching how differently he acts once he has been groomed. When we get him home and inside from the groomers, he immediately runs to the backdoor to be let right back outside. We're pretty sure he likes to go show off his new hairdo to the other dogs in the neighborhood. He's also figured out that he gets a little more love, attention and petting when his hair has been cut. Everyone who sees him tells him how cute he is, and he loves the attention and affection. Humans are the same way. Using good hygiene makes us feel better about ourselves. But when we sort of let ourselves go, it drags us down and affects our mood and how we feel about ourselves. Get into a good routine of personal hygiene. There is nothing like a hot bath or shower at the beginning of the day to get you going or at the end of the day to relax you.

When my kids come home from school or work the first thing their mother has them do is wash their hands and brush their teeth. Son says, "I brushed them this morning!" She says, "Yep that's the problem! They haven't been brushed since this morning!" She says teeth need to be brushed at least 3 times a day. At least! Once they're brushed, they have a nice slick, fresh feel to them, and your breath is on point. This is important because you never know who you are going to run into. This is why I always have my TicTacs with me.

Pets

Speaking of Cooper! Cooper is the "chillest" dog on the planet! There is something about him that helps you relax. He jumps on the sofa with you and hangs out while you pet him. It's almost like he can sense when you need a little extra TLC (tender loving care). Pets are a great source of stress relief. Many military service members are actually prescribed service dogs to help treat post-traumatic stress disorder (PTSD). No matter what, Cooper is always glad to see me. Dogs are known for being nonjudgmental, loyal to their owners and are considered by many to be mankind's best friend. Dogs, however, are not the only pets that may provide stress relief. I mentor a student who has two geckos. She affirms that her geckos have a definite chill factor to them. Caring for them is a healthy exercise that makes her feel needed and appreciated. To be clear, I'm not suggesting that you run out and get a pet! Sometimes owning a pet is not a possibility due to financial or living restraints. You may be able to enjoy a friend or neighbor's pet or perhaps the occasional trip to the pet store or rescue facility can be helpful.

Nutrition

Eating the right foods can also help alleviate stress and anxiety. You can do a quick online search for a list of foods which are believed to have stress-relieving benefits. I didn't list them all here in the book because everyone's taste buds are different. You definitely want to make sure you are getting the proper amount of daily nutrients and not eat too much, or too little.

Journaling

Journaling is one of the best ways to manage stress and anxiety. There is something therapeutic about sitting down and writing your thoughts out on paper. It can be like a brain flush. And once you get it all down, it's like, "There, I said it and I feel better!" I have volumes and volumes of completed journals from writing over the years. Not only is journaling therapeutic, I find it to be very productive. I often use my journal as a reference tool. There is great benefit to looking back at where you were a year prior to see what you were doing at that time. It's helpful in reminding me why I made certain decisions and what was going on inside of me and around me at that time which led to the decision. I learn a lot about myself through journaling. Some of my tendencies are not always the best choices, and journaling helps to me to be aware and make better ones.

Exercise

Exercise is my Go-to-Move for relieving stress! There is never a time when I do a workout that I don't feel better afterwards. When I feel stress coming on, my first move is toward the pull-up bar or the dip machine. When I get tired of a particular workout program, I make changes. I am currently doing calisthenics and running. When I do a good 5-mile run, it feels great! You may think running hurts and I agree, it hurts so good! Not only does exercise lower stress hormones like cortisol, but it also releases endorphins. Endorphins are natural, feel good chemicals your body produces that make you feel better. Develop a healthy exercise program for yourself. It would be a great idea to speak with the physical education teacher at school or a personal trainer. There are so many ways to get the exercise your body needs and you can develop the plan that works best for you!

Stretch and Breathe

Massages are great stress relievers, but they can be very expensive. I have a great low cost exercise that will make you feel better right away. Stretch and Breathe! Close your eyes for a moment and empty your mind of all the things you are thinking and stressing over. Go to a tropical place in your mind or the calming setting of your choice. It may be that you prefer the snowcapped mountains with a beautiful view from the deck of a cabin. Now you are starting to chill for real. Don't fall asleep just yet though. Take a big deep breath and slowly let it out. After a few deep breaths you can ever so gently tilt your head to the left and let the weight of it lightly stretch your neck. Hold it there for a few moments and gently roll it to the right side. Let your head hang in front and then the back. This exercise only takes a few moments but can make a big difference. I am not a personal trainer or yoga instructor by any stretch, so you may want to consult with one or a physician before trying any exercise routine. I know it makes me feel better.

I have a watch that periodically throughout the day reminds me to breathe! When the notification comes up, I have two options. The first option is breathe. When I hit the breathe button, it guides me through a 60-second breathing routine.

At the end of the 60 seconds I always feel better and I'm glad I did it. Not only do I feel better, but it's easy and only takes 60 seconds! The second option is the dismiss button. When I'm "too busy", I hit the dismiss button and keep doing whatever it is I'm doing at that time. I've noticed that every time I hit the dismiss button, it becomes easier to hit the dismiss button the next time and so on. After a while without even intending to, I hit the dismiss button every time and miss out on feeling better. So why is it that something that is so easy to do, and makes me feel better, gets so easily dismissed from my life? Because what is easy to do is just as easy not to do! **When it comes to stress busters we have to be intentional and deliberate in actually using them.** Stress and anxiety are not slacking up on us, so we can't slack off in our approach to managing them either! I often say this to myself out-loud for motivation, "If I can't carve out 60 seconds to breathe in my life, then I don't have much of a life! Pause for 60 seconds and get a life!" That short and powerful conversation with myself is helping to produce big results. JUST BREATHE, JUST CHILLL!

Music

Music can be one of the best tools you can use to relax. When I leave a school from presenting all day, one of the best things I do for myself is put on classical music. Before you knock classical, you need to try it. I stumbled onto this by accident hitting the scan or seek button on the car radio. I was driving along in my car looking for some chill music to unwind and landed on the classical station. I was getting ready to go past it, but, for whatever reason, decided to stop and let it play. I found it to be soothing stuff. I'll ride down the road pretending I am the conductor of the symphony! One hand on the wheel of course and the other hand directing the orchestra. If you spot me on the road you might think I'm crazy. No I'm just in C-H-I-L-L-L mode. The great thing about music is there is some for every occasion. Some music I listen to in order to get hyped and some I listen to in order to relax. Find the music that allows you to chill and let it play.

Singing

I once sang a solo in front of a group of people, and I was never asked to sing again! I'm just not a great singer, so it's a good thing I get paid to speak and not sing. Not being able to sing hasn't stopped me from singing though. I sing in the car going down the road. On special occasions I record a 30-second clip and send it to people as a pick me up or encouragement. I do this on birthdays and holidays for people. It probably does more for me than them, but some of my friends seem to appreciate it. It's actually a lot funnier than it is musically pleasing to the ear. The point is, singing is a great exercise for your lungs and it makes you feel good. Sometimes I make up my own lyrics from tunes of existing songs. Singing is a great way to let it out. Have you some go-to-songs that you enjoy that bring you happiness. When you start to get stressed or anxious, do your own solo performance. It works!

Puzzles

There is nothing like a 500-piece puzzle to take your mind off of everything. You will be so focused on trying to find and connect pieces, that you won't be thinking about the pressures of life. Word searches are awesome for stress relief as well.

Coloring, word-searches, cross-word, painting, etc. I think you get the idea! Having healthy outlets to turn to when you feel stressed equip you with great alternatives to unhealthy habits. I have provided a few for you to consider and putting into practice to help relieve the tension of stress and anxiety.

Action Items and Reminders from Chapter 2

Stress effects everyone, but not everyone's response to managing it is the same. The key is to be aware when stress strikes and have healthy outlets to practice.

1) What situations cause you to stress out and feel anxious?

2) Take a moment and consider any unhealthy approaches you may have to stress and anxiety. What are some unhealthy habits you see in others?

3) Which of the listed healthy outlets, if any, do you think would benefit you?

4) Make a list of 2 or more healthy outlets you can implement when you experience stress.

Chapter 3

Invest in Yourself and the Return in Others

After my daughter's hair fell out, the first thing we did to help her was to make a list of everything she was thankful for (Asset List). The second thing we did was give her a list of things that were awesome about her. I say we gave her a list because she couldn't come up with a list on her own. She was very distraught about the loss of her hair as you can imagine. In addition to struggling with those relationships at school as mentioned earlier, she also dealt with the struggle of wearing a wig and wondering if other people knew she was wearing a wig.

I gave her a notecard and a pen and asked her to write down everything about herself that was really cool. It was upsetting to us when she couldn't come up with even one! So, we gave her a list of 20+ attributes about herself that affirmed her value. She had to get in front of the mirror every night before bed, and every morning when she woke up, and read the list. Within a week she didn't need the notecard. This forced her to look in the mirror as she said those positives things about herself to herself. We saw her confidence and self-worth grow. Her little brother got jealous. He said, "Dad, I want a list!" No problem! We gave him a list, and he would compete for mirror time. He took it to a whole different level transforming into motivational speaker right in front of the mirror! It so happened at that time in his life he was playing recreational baseball. Within a few short weeks of saying his list in the mirror, his batting average rose to number 1 on the team! How could that happen you might ask. Baseball players will tell you that much of what happens at the plate has less to do with mechanics and more to do with what is going on between your ears when you go up to bat. By going up to the plate confident in himself and his ability to hit the ball, he did. The value he had for himself bolstered his value to the team!

My daughter wore a wig for three years. When she turned 15, she took the wig off for good and would you believe it? She had a full head of hair! It went out blonde and came in brown. Her mother and I don't care too much what color it is and neither does she! There are over 80 different colors of hair dye to choose from. I am not saying that the talk in the mirror cured her. I am saying that it helped significantly to reinforce within herself every day for 3 years that she has tremendous value and worth. It helped her take her mind off of her hair loss and things she couldn't control, and focus on the positives and things she could control.

One of the most important conversations you will ever have is the conversation you have with yourself, about yourself, when you are by yourself! Make sure you are having healthy conversations. The conversation you have with yourself on the way to school has a lot to do with the student you are when you get there. The conversation you have with yourself before you take a test has a lot to do with the results of the test or exam (not to mention study and preparation). Also, the conversation you have with yourself before an interview has a lot to do with how well the interview goes. Your internal talk will determine the external results you experience.

Everyone has value

Each and every one has value! Value you can offer other students. Value you can offer your school, family, neighborhood, city, state and beyond. However, one of the biggest challenges I face as I crisscross the country speaking to students is too many students can't see their own value. I asked 5000 students at a career fair assembly, "how many of you consider yourselves to be a salesperson?" Only a few hands were raised. I asked the same group, "How many of you have ever convinced your parents to buy you something?" 5000 hands were raised. I said, "Welcome to the sales department!" The ability to persuade others is of great value! Almost as valuable as the ability to persuade yourself.

I was in the mall with my daughter, and she asked, "Daddy, do you want to go to Starbucks before or after lunch?" Either way, what does she get? Starbucks! Students are absolute geniuses in the way these things are phrased! It wasn't a matter of if we were going to Starbucks, but when. Either way, she's drinking white chocolate macchiato with extra caramel! She definitely has a future in sales. By the way, sales is one of the highest paying professions in the world. The self-value you have now and are currently developing, will also be the value you bring to your future career.

The point is: "You have value!" The value you have is for a purpose! Having purpose gives you hope! Famous speakers John Maxwell and Zig Ziglar said it best, "When there is hope in the future, there is power in the present!" This is so true. You have so much power right now, because you have so much value to put to work toward your purpose. So even if your current situation is hard and you are struggling to get through it, the hope of a brighter future fuels you to keep striving today.

It is a healthy exercise to write down some of the attributes you possess that are of value. It's not an exercise to swell your head or make you into something you are not. You can look in the mirror all day long telling yourself, "I can fly," and it's not going to help you grow wings and get off the ground. This exercise is not to make you arrogant or over confident either. This exercise is meant to uncover or remind yourself that you most certainly have attributes that provide you with the foundation you need to be successful.

Go ahead and get a notecard, and write down as many awesome things about yourself as you can think of. Some who do this exercise will write quickly and need more than one notecard (if this is you, you might want to scale it back a bit). Others will struggle to come up with any at all. You may need someone who can help you with your list. Often times other people can see our value better than we can see it ourselves. If this describes you, then partner with a friend, family member or mentor who can help you discover all of the awesome things about you. When you begin to doubt your value, pull the list out and remind yourself how valuable you really are. It may be helpful to say them out loud and even in front of the mirror. It is like giving yourself your own personal pep talk. It has been said, "The best motivation is self-motivation!" Consider this exercise practicing to be your own personal motivational speaker.

Invest in Yourself

Now that we have established your value, it's time to get busy investing! The best investment you will ever make is the one you make in yourself. Taking the time to think about the things you are thankful for and the list of your valuable attributes is an investment in yourself. You are investing your time and energy into your overall wellness and personal development. Now you want to expand and grow your investment. One of the best investments you can make in yourself is in your own education. The most expensive thing on the planet is ignorance. I have heard it falsely stated many times, "What you don't know won't hurt you." THIS IS A LIE! Simply not knowing something can cost you your finances, relationships, health and even your life if you aren't careful. I could offer multiple examples in my own life and the life of others to illustrate how ignorance has been so very costly. We live in the information age and therefore have no excuse to be ignorant on much of anything. With so much information at our fingertips it is only a matter of caring and valuing yourself enough to make the investment.

In a given school year you are in class 180 days - eight hours per day for a total of 1440 hours - It can feel like a lifetime. The reality is you actually get a total 8760 hours in a year. If you're going to spend 1440 hours in school, then you might as well commit to learning as much as you can while you are there. Make the most of the opportunity! Many students each year go off to college, spend small fortunes in tuition, room, books, fees, etc. only to not show up to class nor milk the professors for everything they know. That is a tremendous waste of resources. Other students see their time in school and college as an investment in themselves, and take advantage of every class and assignment to learn and improve themselves. These students see their teachers and instructors as water and themselves as sponges soaking up every bit of information and experience possible. This will typically be reflected in their grades. Your grades, to an extent, are a reflection of how well you invested the 1440 hours of school time. The other big question is what are you doing with the other 7320? You know! The other 7320 hours when you are not in school. How you invest this time really determines how well you do in school and in life. Being involved in opportunities like student government, student clubs, band, sports, volunteering, part-time jobs, etc. can be great investments. Many lifelong friendships begin by getting involved in these types of productive extra-curricular activities. You don't have to join them all. It is better to join one or two and make a big impact, rather than join a bunch and spread yourself so thin you aren't able to contribute much.

People often ask me where I went to school. My response: I have a bachelor's degree from the University of South Carolina, a master's degree from The School of Hard Knocks (toughest program in the world) and a Ph.D. from WSU (Wind-

Shield University). If I am driving my car, looking through the windshield, or flying on a plane, I more often than not am listening to podcasts, books, seminars, and lectures. That is some of the best time to self-educate and invest in my personal and professional development. I especially enjoy podcasts because you can listen **FOR FREE** to content experts who make $20,000 - $40,000 per lecture! (If it's free, it's me!) It has been suggested that, if you were to ride or drive 12,000 or more miles per year, you could get the equivalent of a college degree in a few short years simply by listening to right information. Make the most of your windshield time.

Re-Invest in Others

As you invest in yourself, you are going to be presented with opportunities to re-invest your growth and development (your return) into others! This is such an exciting benefit of self - investment. You will be surprised how people will begin to take notice of how well you are doing! It will be obvious to them that while others are worried, stressed and anxious, you seem to be cool, calm and collected. You may even have people begin to ask you for advice. This will be your opportunity to invest your return in others.

When you go through a particular struggle, heartache or traumatic event, it comes with the benefit of experience. Whether it's the death of a close friend, divorce of parents, eviction from home, change of schools, etc., your perseverance and triumph through these circumstances prepares you to help someone else go through the same type of experience. Some of the things I faced as a student uniquely position me to help others go through similar things.

When I was nine years old my parents divorced, and Dad pretty much disappeared. I jokingly called him Houdini because he did a disappearing act on us. The problem is he forgot the 2nd part of the act, reappearing. It was one of the toughest times in my life for me and my family. You don't fully understand these things that happen that are out of your control at the time. You often have more questions than answers. I don't fully understand now to be quite honest. However, I do know what it is like to go through it and can certainly relate to someone going through a similar situation. I have had the opportunity to be an encouragement to many students whose parents have divorced and students who have experienced abandonment. The crazy thing is each and every time I get that type of opportunity it helps me as well. Part of my continued healing is closely related to helping others heal. This is the beauty of investing in others! It is the compounding effect! If you know anything about finances, you know Albert Einstein considered compounding interest to be the 8th wonder of the world. Investing in other people has a compounding effect for the investor. Each time you help someone along life's way it helps you more than it helps them. Not only that, perhaps the person you helped goes on to help someone else, and so on. Who knows how many lives you will impact by investing in yourself and the return in others.

Let them Breathe

I do want to offer a piece of advice when helping others through a tough time. Give them a moment to catch their breath. I remember playing on the playground as a kid and having the wind knocked out of me. Everyone would rush up and crowd around, when what I really needed was a small moment of space to catch my breath. Once I caught my breath, it was nice to have a hand up. It's like that with helping a friend through a tough time. You give them a moment to catch their breath, and then extend the hand to help them up and through it.

The writing of this book is an investment of my return into others. My hope is that it helps the reader and, in turn, the reader is better positioned and inspired to help others and so on. Giving of your time, treasure and talent is one of the most rewarding and stress relieving exercises you can do. Every time I give out of what I have to someone or a great cause it feels so good. I call it giving living! It makes for a great hashtag! #givingliving.

My son volunteered several times during his summers in high school with a program called Camp Joy. Each time he spent a week as the counselor of a special needs camper. One week he had a camper who "never" slept, so my son didn't either! The one time he did fall asleep, his camper woke him up yelling with an entire bottle of shampoo in his hair and eyes because he decided to shower in the middle of the night. It is the least amount of sleep he has ever gotten over a one-week period, and yet the most rewarding. The highlight of the week is the talent show where campers display the unique gifts and skills sets they have. It is an entertaining and moving event.

I am of the firm belief that you don't have to look very far to find need. You can volunteer at a local community center or food bank. My family and I had the chance to participate in a one-day clinic for the unsheltered. Unsheltered is another way of saying homeless. The unsheltered visited the outdoor event and secured much needed food and hygiene products. They got haircuts, manicures and help in getting personal identification documents. We spent the majority of the time that day simply listening to their stories. This is where the biggest difference was made. It did a lot for them, knowing someone does care and that they are wanted and not forgotten. All it costs us was our time. If you can't afford to give anything out of your pocket, you can still volunteer your time. Giving living not only makes you feel good, it also makes a difference in the lives of others.

4 Types of Students

It's been said by others and myself that there are 3 types of students: those who make it happen, those who watch it happen and those who say, "What Happened?" It is a funny saying and partially correct. I went to school with really 4 types of students and you may recognize these at your school.

First Type: Those trying to "get around" it. Some students would spend more energy getting out of school, assignments and homework than if they would have put the work in.

Second Type: Those who "get through" it. They do the minimum required because all their trying to do is get through the day, week, semester, school year. They never really put forth their best effort and usually see minimal results.

Third Type: Those who "get from" it. These students absorb everything they can. They are outstanding at studying and delivering top notch work to make great grades and perform well on standardized tests in an effort to get into the post-secondary schools of their choice.

Fourth Type: Those who "give" to it. These students are truly amazing and exceptional. They see the school as theirs and try to leave a legacy for the students coming behind them. They may or may not be at the top of the class academically, but in terms of school spirit and investing in the school, they are second to none. These students in the end get far more from their school experience than any of the others because of how much they give to it. These students are in position to have a tremendous impact on the overall culture at their schools. You can too!

You are your best investment

The best investment you will ever make is the investment you make in yourself! It is necessary to invest in yourself first so you are better equipped and prepared to invest the return in others. A good illustration occurs in air travel. I flew over 57 flights last year. Without exception every flight begins with passenger instructions from the flight crew. (I have noticed that very few people pay attention during this time). The crew lets us know in the event of a loss of cabin pressure, oxygen masks will fall from the ceiling. Once the masks drop, we are instructed to put it on our faces and pull the strap to hold it in place. The oxygen will begin to flow. Then they are sure to include that, if we have small children with us on the plane, "BE SURE TO PUT YOUR MASK ON FIRST!" If a passenger doesn't put his or her mask on first, then they may not have the oxygen they need to help the children. If a passenger tries to put a child's mask on first, then he or she may pass out in the process. Much like the example of the oxygen mask on the plane, we have to make sure we take care of our own needs so we can be better positioned to help others. The return you invest in others is the better equipped healthier you, pouring back into others.

Make a commitment today to invest in yourself. It's easy to get complacent about school especially as the year can seemingly drag on, but you can't afford to let it slip. You are too valuable an investment not to make sure you are getting everything you need. Once you are seeing yourself as an investment and making great decisions, then its time to pay attention to what every investor watches: ROI (return on investment) A healthier, stress-free you is going to be in great position to excel and invest in others. It will all begin to come together for you.

Reminders and Action Items from Chapter 3

You have tremendous value! The best investment you can make is in your own education and personal development. As you develop your value appreciates and you want to be sure to invest your return into others.

1) Make an honest list of all of your valuable attributes.

2) When you find yourself doubting or needing a confidence boost read your list to yourself.

3) Re-invest your value. Whether it be your school, neighborhood or a friend in need, be sure to give back and invest in others.

Chapter 4

Lean on Others

After my parents divorced and dad went MIA (missing in action), it left a void in the home. Even though he wasn't around much before, it was even worse after he left. It was my good fortune to have a Boys and Girls Club in my neighborhood. My mom signed me and my brothers up to attend after school and during the summer. I was not too terribly excited because I hadn't heard the best things about the place, which turned out to not be true at all.

When I walked into the club for the first time, it was pretty exciting. They had an indoor basketball court and a games room with ping pong, pool table and foosball table (great outlets for stress and anxiety). They also had a media center and a canteen to buy snacks! I loved playing the games and competing in tournaments. I became an excellent ping pong player and a pretty good baller as well.

It wasn't the games, though, that brought me back every day nor the reason they had to run me out of the place at night. I was what they called an every day all day member. I was at the club from the time the doors opened until the placed closed. The real reason I was going there so much was their staff working there. They were investing in us, teaching us accountability and to not make excuses for ourselves or allow anyone else to make excuses for us. I learned to not blame dad's leaving on anything, but to flip it around and use it as motivation to get from where I was to where I wanted to be in life. The staff members were validating us and showing us affection that we were starving for. I learned to lean on them during hard times and have difficult conversations when I needed a listening ear. Mr. David, the club director, became a mentor to me.

When I was 13 years old the staff at the club approached me with a request. They shared that they needed to raise money and awareness for the programs at the club and asked me to tell my story at the board meeting the next morning. I declined, assuring them they had the wrong guy.

The conversation went like this:

> Staff: "We want you to talk about your club experience at our board meeting."
>
> Me: "I don't do speeches! You should get someone else."
>
> Staff: "If you do it, you'll get a sausage biscuit from Hardees!"
>
> Me: "What time y'all picking me up?"

The biscuit did it for me! You have to understand that we rarely had the opportunity to eat restaurant food. We ate breakfast at school as well as lunch and whatever my mom managed to get on the table for supper! Sausage biscuit from Hardees!? Sign me up!

They picked me up outside of my house the next morning and drove me in to downtown Columbia, SC. We went in an office building and onto the elevator to get to the 2nd floor. When I walked into the boardroom, I saw the longest table ever. There were all of these important people sitting around it, and I could tell they were successful by looking at them. I was getting nervous.

I looked over and noticed the table against the wall was loaded with biscuits. I headed towards the table with the thought of calming my nerves with a biscuit. As I headed towards the biscuits, they asked me what I was doing. I said, "I'm going to get a biscuit." They said, "You get the biscuit after you give the speech!" I could see the biscuits and smell them. This was a powerful incentive. With my mouth watering, I gave the speech of a lifetime telling them all of the exciting things we were doing at the club every day; how the staff members at the club were helping us with homework and school projects, and how to manage difficult situations in life. When I was done sharing, something happened that I cannot remember ever happening up to that point in my life. All of these important, successful people began to clap! I had never received applause before, and it felt good! They didn't give me just one biscuit. They gave me two biscuits! I said, "When is the next board meeting? I'll be back!" I made it a goal that one day I would be one of those people sitting at that boardroom table. It happened!

By the time I was 15, I was travelling with the club. I became a member of a club within the Boys and Girls Club called Keystone Club. It consisted of members with officers whose primary focus was providing leadership to younger members through volunteering. (I wonder where I got the idea of investing in self and the return in others?). The Keystone Club held state, regional and national conferences. When I was in the 10th grade, they took a group of us up to Pittsburgh, PA to attend the National Keystone Conference of approximately 1200 members from around the country. We got to meet members from California, Texas and New York. For most of us it was the first time we had ever been out of the state of South Carolina and the first time we had stayed in a hotel. And not just any hotel, but the William Penn Hotel! It was amazing, overwhelming and a bit intimidating, but what an awesome opportunity and experience. There is a picture of the group we took on the "about" page of my website at brooksharper.com. I'll give you 30 seconds to find me in the photo.

They took us to a fancy Italian restaurant in downtown Pittsburgh. The only thing we knew about Italian food was pizza and SpaghettiOs. Most of us ordered pizza (It was the safe choice), with the exception of one of the guys in our group. In an effort to rise to the occasion, he pretended to be fancy. He called the waiter over, pointed at the menu and in a sophisticated voice and said, "What is this?" The waiter said, "Sir, that is Linguini." He said, "Then that's what I want." The food came, and we devoured our pizza. Our fancy friend just stared at his plate as the linguini began to congeal. You could tell by the look on his face; he was disappointed. We asked, "Why aren't you eating?" He said, "I'm not eating because this is not linguini!" We said, "What is it?" He said, "Noodles!" We laughed so hard, but the truth is we had no idea that linguini is simply a fancy name for noodles. We learned all of this, because these folks were investing in us. Through our involvement and these experiences, they were exposing us to culture and cuisine that we would otherwise have known nothing about.

Learn to Lean

The guy who was making all of this happen for us was my mentor I mentioned earlier, Mr. David. We called him "Dave Money". Even though he wasn't really rich, he was money in our books. He was a bridge for us. A bridge takes you from where you are to where you need to be. Mr. David was taking us from country to cultured, and from ignorant to informed. He saw something in us before we could see it in ourselves; assuring us we could be far more than we ever imagined.

We were learning to LEAN! We were learning to lean on the right people for support and guidance. It's not an easy thing to do sometimes. Especially if you've been hurt and have a hard time trusting people. However, because we saw Mr. David going the extra mile for us, we trusted him to help us get there.

Sometimes we need that lift from someone else. Too often in our effort to be self-reliant and unburdening to others, we allow ourselves to fall further down to our own detriment. There is nothing to be embarrassed about or wrong about leaning on others for help. Whatever the situation is, no matter how stressed or depressed you might be, find someone to lean on for support to get you through. You may think you are alone; YOU'RE NOT! You may think it's too late; IT'S NOT! You may think no one will understand what you're going through; THEY WILL! You may think there isn't any hope; THERE IS!

Just like you don't have to look far to discover folks in need, likewise you don't have to look far to find someone to lean on in your own need! It is perfectly normal to need help and perfectly fine to ask for help. Many overwhelmed, struggling college students wait until the last week before the semester ends to ask their professors for help; only to discover their professors are far more approachable and helpful than they ever believed. The professors keep regular office hours with the specific goal of meeting with students and offering assistance when they get stuck. After students finally meet with the professor, they can't believe how easy the conversation ended up being, and regret not asking for help sooner.

The 2 keys to leaning on others:

1. Lean on the right person(s) - Make sure it's someone you trust, like a parent, grand parent, school counselor or mentor. Be cautious about sharing your struggles with just any and everyone who will listen. Some people won't hold what you tell them in confidence. They may put your business out there or perhaps even use it against you.

2. Lean early – Be proactive in your approach to seeking support. When you sense things beginning to weigh on

you and find yourself becoming anxious, lean on your support system sooner rather than later. Lean on the action steps that you have learned in this book. Waiting until things pile up on you before employing support or proven techniques, can make it that much harder to get back to normal.

When we don't lean on others for support, not only do we not get the help we need, we also rob that person of the opportunity to be a help. We rob them of the joy and benefit that comes from helping someone else. I was at a school speaking and had a conversation with a student after the presentation. He shared he was having a tough year and was starting to turn the corner, and how much he appreciated me visiting the school. Afterwards the counselor thanked me for taking a moment to speak with him. She also shared that some folks in the community knew his family was struggling financially and tried to provide some relief, but his parents refused to accept the help though it was desperately needed. The family was too embarrassed to allow anyone to help them. We all need help at some point in our lives and it is certainly okay to receive it.

Think for a moment about the greatest accomplishment you could ever achieve. What, for you, would be the ultimate achievement? For some it may be President of the United States, CEO of a major company, or to hit a walk-off grand slam at the World Series. All of these would be tremendous victories. But one of the greatest accomplishments or awards anyone can receive is to make an appearance in someone else's story. Perhaps one day one of your friends, students or even patients gets up to tell their story about how they were close to giving up or in some sort of great need and just at the right time, you offered a word of encouragement or helping hand that made the difference. It is going to be one of the greatest feelings you ever experience.

It may be that you have already appeared in someone's story and even multiple people. That's awesome! But it would only be possible if that person allows you to help them. Wouldn't it be sad if you were able to make a big difference in the life of a person you care about, but they wouldn't let you?   You would probably be frustrated. Well, It is the same way when you need help and don't ask or allow a trusted person to help you. If and when you need help be sure to ask and ask early!

Reminders and Action Items from Chapter 4

It's is a good thing to have trustworthy people in your circle to lean on in times of need. It is perfectly okay to ask for help when you need it.

1) Lean on the right person(s)

2) Lean early. Don't wait until you are in dire straits to ask for help.

3) Think about someone who has helped you in some way and write the story of how their influence impacted your life.

Chapter 5

Let Loose

Let loose doesn't mean to go crazy, releasing your inhibitions. Let loose means letting go of things that are causing us stress and anxiety. I've heard many people tell the story of how spider monkeys are trapped by hunters, so I am unsure who to give the credit to for this powerful illustration. The story goes like this: The hunter hollows out a coconut and nails it to the tree, and then drops a shiny pebble or marble into the coconut. The spider monkey, being a curious creature, climbs the tree and looks into the coconut and discovers the shiny object. He has to have it, so he reaches in and grabs a hold of it and, now, is faced with a dilemma. His hand has made a fist too big to pull through the opening of the coconut. In his frustration he tugs, screams and goes bananas to get his hand and pebble loose. This signals the hunter to come and trap him. The monkey has two choices at this point. He can let go and escape or hold on and be captured. Unfortunately, in most cases the spider monkey refuses to let loose and is captured.

We are a lot like the spider monkey. We often hold on to things to our own detriment. Rather than letting loose and moving on, we hold on at a great cost to our health and well-being. Our burden gets heavier and heavier until the sheer weight of it causes us to spiral downward into a dangerous place. Below is a list of things you might consider letting loose of in an effort to lighten your load, and manage some of the things that are potentially weighing you down.

Let Loose of:

Grudges

Let loose of Grudges. At some point in life, we're done wrong or slighted! Someone does or says something that brings us pain and grief, and I'm sure you, like me, can give many examples. We all can relate to this, but we all don't respond the same. Some people forgive and move on, while others hold grudges and become bitter. Nelson Mandela famously said, "Resentment is like drinking poison and expecting your enemies to die." Grudges really only hurt the person who holds them. The person we hold the grudge against is probably getting a great night sleep, while we lose sleep stewing over what they did. That makes us even more frustrated, and, if we are not careful, we can get very bitter.

The tip I have for you in these types of situations is to **Lead with Love!** I mean practice forgiving people before it happens. This might sound crazy, and it is certainly easier said than done. Leading with love is about understanding in advance that people are going to make mistakes, both accidentally and sometimes purposely. They may say the wrong thing or share something that you told them in secret. Understanding that people mess up, you can go ahead and cut them slack in advance. The truth is we all mess up sometimes and need another chance. I know I have! If you yourself want another chance when you mess up, then you should be willing to give others another chance. Let me be clear, leading with love doesn't mean we turn into a doormat or punching bag to be abused. That is certainly not healthy! If you find this is the case, you add distance to the equation. Meaning you forgive and then distance yourself from the reach and influence of that person.

When my parents divorced, I experienced a wide range of emotions: anger, sadness, disbelief. It was even more surreal as it became increasingly obvious that my dad was not coming back around. But I had to move forward. I couldn't stay stuck there. People would say things like, "There is good that comes out of every situation." That sounded like the most ridiculous statement I had ever heard. How could anything good come out of this? Sometimes it's better to say nothing at all than say something ridiculous. Years went by. I graduated from high school, then college, got married, had children, and then my dad mysteriously popped back up on the grid. He surfaced with a terminal illness, homeless, and my older brother took him in for a period of time. I flew my family to meet the father-in-law and grandad they had never met. I spent a week with him listening to his side of things leading with love the entire way. Much of what he said didn't make any sense and sounded more like excuses than owning what he did. I noticed his philosophies on life were very different from mine. As I flew back home, I had a moment of clarity. When those people years before said that good would come from my situation, I finally was able to get my mind around it. Good did come. I understood that it was good thing for me that I wasn't exposed to his philosophies growing up. Closure! Just like that, I had reconciled the entire thing in my heart and mind. It took a long time to get a better understanding, and I am so glad that I had decided to let loose of the grudge as a child instead of holding on to it for all of those years. Sometimes the struggle makes you stronger!

Payback

Let loose of payback. There is an old saying: "What goes around comes around!" This means what people do to others eventually comes back around to them, whether it be positive or negative. Payback takes care of itself, so there is no need to make revenge a goal. Let loose of payback and let payback do its thing. There is a legendary feud between two families called the Hatfields and McCoys. Some say it started over a simple misunderstanding, while others say that not even the families know how it started. It became a lifelong fight of payback between two families it escalated in severity with each blow leading to bloodshed and even death. Imagine being in a fight that long and not even knowing what you are fighting over. Talk about exhausting! Instead of one side leading with love and letting payback take care of itself, they each insisted on "one upping" the other, costing them things they could never recover.

Author and speaker, John Maxwell, says, "I can't control how people respond to me. I can only control how I respond to people." I have learned that if you accept this truth and respond appropriately, it brings a lot more peace and happiness into your life. It also helps lower your stress and anxiety level. The truth is people are sometimes going to let you down and disappoint you in their response. Sometimes people mess with you just so they can provoke a response from you! Don't follow it up! Let loose.

I was travelling to speak at a school way out in the country. You would call it the middle of nowhere. I got to a stop sign and pulled up behind another car. We were both turning right. Apparently, I got too close to the other driver's car. I found this out after turning right and passing the other car. Several miles down the road I could sense something on my right going on in my peripheral vision. When I looked over, I saw the other driver yelling at me with both of his arms out of the window. I am not sure how he was steering his car! I couldn't hear a word he was saying, so I put the window down. That's when I heard him yelling at the top of his lungs, "You got too close to my bumper! I've got high blood pressure! My daughter...."

PAUSE – This is where things can get out of hand! Have you ever heard of road rage? That's when people get so upset with other drivers that they lose control of themselves, all sense of reason goes out of the window, and they commit violence which is way out of their normal character. Now, I can't control how this man is responding to me getting "too close" to his bumper or how high his blood pressure is. All I can control is how I'm going to respond to this man yelling at me with both his hands out the window. I can be calm or match his level of intensity. In real time, situations like this are happening so fast that usually reflexes take over. Our reflexes don't always make the best choices, especially if you are used to popping off at the slightest thing. I am by nature a pretty laidback person and stay calm in the chaos. I quickly decided to attempt defusing the situation.

I said, "I'm sorry, sir! I'm not from here, and I'm looking for the high school". And just like that his whole demeanor changed! He turned into the sweetest old dude you would ever know. He said, "Oh, you're looking for the high school? Follow me!"

I got behind him and followed him all the way to the school. He pulled in and pointed to the door I needed to go in, wished me well, and then pulled off. As far as I know, I've never seen him again and probably never will. I was so glad he wasn't the principal! The point is the response. Instead of escalating the intensity, I chose to chill, let loose, and ended up with a much better result. Who knows? That man could have had a heart attack if he hadn't calmed down. Then I would have felt really bad.

When you find yourself in intense situations, remind yourself that you can only control your response and commit to having the best response. Payback is a poor motivator for doing anything. Let Payback take care of itself.

Things That Don't Belong to You

Let loose of things that don't belong to you! This is not about returning things that have been found or borrowed, rather it's about not picking up other people's drama which has nothing to do with you. Some students and even adults, think it's their life's mission to insert themselves into other people's business. They justify their unnecessary involvement by saying things like: "That's my friend..." If it's really a friend, you may not be helping by escalating and intensifying their situation. A true friend focuses on the friend, not on inserting themselves into the fray.

I know two students who were dating for quite a while and then they broke up. In his frustration, he posted a picture of her smiling on social media with a nasty caption. Not a wise thing to do. As soon as I saw it, I shook my head and said, "Here we go!" I didn't touch it or even go near it! I knew my involvement would only make it worse, but there were plenty of other people who unnecessarily picked up the drama even though it didn't belong to them!

SOCIAL MEDIA IS A POWERFUL TOOL, BUT A VERY POOR WEAPON!

It can be hard to leave these things alone. The urge to pick up the cause is so tempting. I've learned that Social Media is not the best forum for airing grievances. Though it can be so inviting and expedient, it often ends up doing more harm than good. Social Media is a powerful tool but a very poor weapon. There are times when it is the right thing to defend someone and engage, but social media is not the forum for the conversation. You will get so much more by having a real conversation as opposed to a social media conversation.

SOMETIMES THE BEST RESPONSE IS NO RESPONSE!

The truth is sometimes the best response is no response! Not responding to things which don't belong to you, can have a more powerful result. Not responding shows you are not going to fall for the trap being set. Not responding is taking the high road instead of going down into the mud. When you go down into the mud to wrestle with the pigs, you eventually figure out that the pigs like it!

Here is a phrase to commit to memory:

Don't Sweat the Petty or Pet the Sweaty!

The "petty" are the small things that get blown up into big things. It's the little things in life that eat us up from the inside out. Its kind of like a constant drip on a rock that doesn't do much to the rock in the short term, but in the long term wears it down to nothing. Let loose of the petty things. Don't allow small nuisances to throw you off your game. Stay focused on the important things and keep them as the priority of your time, energy and effort. The "sweaty" are the people who try to suck you into their negative world! They bait you with silly comments that don't deserve a response or room in your head. Don't sweat them by pouring your energy into their energy sucking world. Don't allow the petty to rent free space in your head.

PICK YOUR BATTLES

When it comes to digital and social media, here is my best advice:

1. Face problems, don't Facebook them
2. Be discreet when you Tweet
3. Pause before you post
4. Count to 10 before you hit send. You may need to count to 110.

F.O.G

Let loose of FOG! Another way to say it is come out of the FOG! FOG stands for fear, obligation and guilt, all of which can produce massive amounts of stress and anxiety in our lives. I bundled these together into an acronym to make it easier to remember it, identify it and respond appropriately when you find yourself in the FOG. It is not uncommon for students to use FOG to manipulate other students into giving them what they want or into behaving a particular way. FOG is the absolute favorite tool of peer pressure! If another student is using FOG to pressure you in any way, then they are definitely not your friend or operating in your best interest. Sometimes you can be in the FOG and not even realize it. I will address fear, obligation, and guilt individually below.

Fear – Fear is being afraid to do, or not do, something because of what may, or may not, happen if you do, or don't, comply. I know that is a mouthful. Simply put, You shouldn't have to do anything because you are afraid to or afraid not to. If another student tells you that if you don't do a certain thing then something will happen to you, then they are using fear in an attempt to control you. If you feel threatened in any way, this is a clear indication that fear is being used against you. This type of pressure in your life creates a hostile, stressful environment, and it is very unhealthy.

Performing at your best is hard enough, as it is, without also having fear to deal with. You don't have to live in fear. If you feel threatened or pressured in any form or fashion, ask for help. Go to that trusted person you lean on, whom we discussed in the previous chapter, and tell them what is going on.

3 Fears to Let Loose:

Fear of Failure – Don't let the fear of failing keep you from trying! Sometimes you win and sometimes you learn! Failing can be one of the best learning experiences. Each time you fail you get a bit wiser and better prepared for the next attempt. Your attitude towards falling down is so important! If you do come up short, cut yourself some slack. You aren't going to ace every exam in school or in life, and that is ok. Michael Jordan was in a famous commercial where he listed many of his failures: the number of shots he had missed, games lost, etc. He said, "I have failed over and over and over again in my life, and that is why I succeed." Our failures can be the greatest lessons and most powerful motivators if we make the most of them.

Fear of Success – Successes are meant to be celebrated not avoided! It may sound crazy that someone would be afraid of winning, but some people are. They don't want the pressure and shine that come with being number 1, because it pushes them out of their comfort zone. Lean into the discomfort if this describes you. The benefits of succeeding far outweigh the comfort of mediocrity.

Fear of Missing Out (FOMO) – FOMO can make you LOCO! You can't be everywhere all of the time! Sometimes in life we have to settle for hearing about it rather than experiencing it. It's Cool! You're going to be sharing the story of your experience with your friends when they miss out. Some of the best fortune I've had in my life came from missing out. When I was in high school The Rolling Stones brought their "Steel Wheels Tour" to South Carolina. They were scheduled to play in the football stadium of Clemson University which was a couple of hours away from my school. Around that same time we had a new student at school who had an inside connection to get concert tickets. This immediately skyrocketed her popularity. Everyone who was going gave her their money to secure the tickets. People who weren't even planning to go originally, now had purchased tickets through her. I was not one of them for two reasons: 1) no money, 2) no way my mom was letting me go to a Rolling Stones Concert in Clemson. Missing out is a bummer right? On the day of the concert everyone showed up at school to get their tickets for that evening, except the new student. She wasn't there! Everyone was in a frenzy trying to locate her. By 3:00 that afternoon it was starting to become painfully obvious that she wasn't showing up with the tickets. Not only did she not show up with the tickets, she never showed back up at school again! She totally disappeared with the money. The only thing I missed out on was getting scammed! You don't have to be afraid of missing out. You can't do it all, and that's ok. Let loose!

Side Note: Fear and respect are not the same. For instance, I am not afraid of driving, but I wear my seat belt out of respect for the dangers that come with driving. Using caution out of respect for safety isn't the same thing as doing something out of fear. I want to be clear here so you don't misunderstand what is being said about fear. I don't want you to throw caution and prudence out the window, because you confuse them with what is being said about fear. Healthy respect can be a very powerful motivator!

Obligation – Obligation is doing something because you feel like you owe it to someone else. Always be careful about what you commit and obligate yourself to. When I was in college I ran up a ton of credit card debt due to my financial ignorance and inability to say no to myself and others. I over obligated myself financially, and it was extremely difficult to pay it off.

Have you ever felt like someone did something for you in an effort to obligate you to do something for them? It could be a situation where you didn't ask the person to do it, but as soon as they did they requested something from you. It's as if they only did it because they wanted something from you. Sometimes it comes in the form of a compliment. If that is the case then they weren't being generous or genuine at all, they were being deceptive. When you do something out of obligation, it's not going to be as effective or powerful because the motivation is wrong. Motive for doing what we do has a lot to do with how well we do it. When we do something because we are obligated, we don't have that same drive to perform.

Guilt – is being made to feel bad or regretful if you don't comply. The last trip you want to be on is a guilt trip. If someone said to you, "If you were my friend, then you would do this for me" and so you do it because you feel guilty of not being a good friend if you don't. The truth is if that person was really your "friend", then they wouldn't use guilt to get something from you.

Guilt isn't always something that others impose on us. Sometimes we apply guilt to ourselves, and it can haunt us for a long time. The previous chapter talked about learning to lead with love and cut others some slack, but we also need to know how to love ourselves and cut ourselves some slack. It is ok to forgive yourself for making mistakes! We all make mistakes from time to time and we want to use them as a learning tool but not as a means to continually punish ourselves. There are some things I have said and done in my lifetime that I would like to have a do over. Unfortunately, I cannot take those things back. I can, however, ask for forgiveness, and forgive myself. I don't have to let regrets cripple me from moving forward and you don't either. When you mess up, say, "I messed up!" Apologize to others and yourself where necessary, learn from it and move forward.

FOG is never a good reason to do anything. I have wanted to write this book for quite some time but had a difficult time getting started. There were events happening in my community and beyond that compelled me to finally start writing. I enjoy seeing students succeed and hope this book will help students across the country manage the stress and anxiety that can be so inhibiting. But if I was writing this book out of fear, obligation or guilt, it wouldn't have the same vibe or impact that it is going to have.

I have been in the FOG in my life. I have had people who I thought were my friends use FOG as a tool to manipulate me. I was an easy target as I think about it, because I like to please people and don't want to let anyone down. It is such a freeing feeling to be out of the FOG!

The thing about FOG is it can creep in without you even realizing it, and all of a sudden you can't see what's really happening. Can you think of instances where you have been in the FOG? Are you in the FOG now? If so, come up with a plan to get out of the FOG. You may need to go to the people you LEAN on for help. They can be like a lighthouse for you in guiding you out of the FOG.

The "Joneses"

Let loose of the "Joneses." "Keeping up with the Joneses" is an expression from an old cartoon strip. The "Joneses" represent the family in a neighborhood that people try to keep up with. If the Joneses get a new car, the neighbors, in an effort to stay in the same socio-economic class, are compelled to get a new car as well. When the Joneses have a new pool put it their yard, other families follow suit. There is no end to it, it's exhausting and not everyone can afford to keep up. Some families find themselves in dire financial trouble in an effort to stay on par with everyone else.

When a student at your school gets the latest phone or similar "must have" item, other students see it and want it too. They go home and put pressure on their parents to get them one, because they don't want to be left behind. They don't want to be "the only student" who doesn't have the latest release. This happens with all sorts of products and events. We are constantly paying attention to what is "trending" and trying to stay up to speed at all cost. It's exhausting, never ending, and stressful! Let loose of the Joneses and what is trending. Let them be them and you be you.

When I was in middle school all of the students in my school were wearing a particular style shirt. Everyone seemed to be so judgmental of the clothes other students were wearing, and you weren't considered cool if you didn't have them. The problem for me and my brothers was my mom couldn't afford the popular brands. I wore hand-me-down clothes throughout middle school and high school. Mom would go to thrift stores like Goodwill and buy used name brand clothes. She would take the labels and emblems off of the name brand clothes and sew them on and in our clothes. No one knew the difference! The reality is on many of the clothes we wear, and other products we purchase, there is no difference in the quality of the brand name and off brand. People pay more for the name. In the end it doesn't matter what other people think. Many people go broke trying to keep up with the Joneses. I'm a pretty competitive person when it comes to sports and games, but not when it comes to status symbols and stuff. I've seen so many people buy things they don't need with money they don't have to keep up with people they don't even necessarily like. It's pointless, expensive and exhausting. Let loose of the Joneses, and, while you're at it, let loose of what other people think.

Devices

Let Loose of Devices. Sometimes we just need to unplug! Put down the phone, the pad, the laptop and take a break from the constant stimulation! I didn't say get rid of them! Don't panic or run away on me. Don't start hiding your phone from me! I'm not taking anything from you. I'm only suggesting that our devices sometimes become vices that squeeze some of the life out of us. Being constantly engaged with the screen can be draining and the source of some of the stress and anxiety in our lives. Too much screen time right before you go to bed has been proven to have a negative impact on our ability to fall and stay asleep. Studies show that the screen puts off the same blue light that the sun puts off. When the sun goes down our bodies release natural melatonin that causes us to feel sleepy. If we are getting blue light, however, from our phones at night our bodies don't release the melatonin at the same levels, if at all. This could be impacting that good night's rest we need.

In addition, devices can steal away cool moments with the most important people around us. We miss the good fun we can have by being distracted by meaningless screen time that can be looked at later. I was out to dinner recently with my wife and noticed another couple across from us eating dinner. They never looked at each other or even spoke, but were buried in their phones the entire meal. Wherever you are, whatever you are involved in, be there and be engaged. Don't be distracted by your device. Let loose.

Clutter

Let loose of clutter! It may sound redundant to say let loose of clutter since everything mentioned so far is potentially cluttering your mind and life. I recently read an article that stated 25% of people with 2 car garages have no room to park the cars because of all their clutter! They park their vehicles worth tens of thousands of dollars in the elements to keep all of the junk protected!? The reality is we accumulate a massive amount of stuff without even realizing it. It becomes painfully obvious if you ever have to move because everything has to be packed and unpacked, and you're like, "where did I get all of this stuff?" The more things we accumulate, the smaller our space seems to get and that can begin to add stress to our lives. We try to find something we need and have a hard time getting our hands on it because it's hidden by much of what we don't need. If you try to inventory everything you own, it might shock you how much you have. It may be time to make room by reducing the amount of things that you have. I decided at the beginning of the year to try and part with one thing a day for the entire year. It was much more difficult than I thought it would be. I have a lot of stuff! I'm thinking, "this will be easy!" For the first few weeks it was! I was getting rid of things I hadn't used or even considered in years that were taking up space in my world. I made multiple trips to Goodwill, the dump and was able to convert some of my trash to cash through the sale of items. About four months into the process, it became more and more difficult to let go of things, and I stopped around the 5-month mark. The pandemic (COVID 19) slowed my willingness to let go of things, thinking I might need these at a later date because of lack of availability. For those five months, though, it felt really good to say goodbye to some things that had served me well and allow them to be repurposed and benefit someone else.

It is so easy for our stuff to pile up on us over time, and we don't even realize how the clutter bogs us down, potentially causing anxiety and limiting our ability to function efficiently. Consider a cell phone with limited storage. As it reaches its storage capacity, it performs slower and slower until it can hardly function. All of a sudden it can barely perform the simplest of commands. Similarly, we can be overloaded with so many trinkets, we feel we don't have space to do anything. It may be time to take the inventory challenge and repurpose some of your unnecessary items taking up your space.

Decluttering can free up space and make it easier to organize your life. Having less to keep up with makes the organization process easier. You'll find that the more organized you become in one area of your life, like clutter, can improve organization in other areas of your life such as time. Organization can be a great stress reliever, knowing you have your mind around your responsibilities and your life is put together.

I'm not suggesting you let loose of something that is of major significance or sentimental value that you will later regret. You would be letting loose of one thing only to replace it with a different type of weight, regret. I am suggesting the most important things in life are not things! The most important things are relationships and the experiences with those relationships. Besides, it feels really good to take something you don't need any more and give it to someone who does. One person's junk becomes another person's treasure! This gives you a double positive! Win-Win situations like this make you feel great!

This is how I've always done it

Let loose of "this is how I've always done it!" Change happens whether we like it or not. They say that the only individuals who actually like change are babies with their diapers. They cry to be changed. The rest of us cry to not change. Change is hard because it can be painful and push us out of our comfort zone. You may have already tried to implement some changes to how you manage stress since reading this book and found it quite difficult. Some of them are harder than others. However, the pain of change can be far less severe than the pain caused by not changing.

It is by far my preference to speak in front of live audiences! I like to interact and draw energy from the crowd, but that is not an option right now because we are in a pandemic. I have had to learn to be effective as I can be virtually, so I can continue to deliver my message.

Things you cannot control

Let loose of things you cannot control! This will drive you crazy more than any other thing. Your life will be exceptionally easier the sooner you are able to figure out what you can and cannot control, and let loose of the latter. You cannot control people for instance. You might be able to influence or persuade someone, but not control them. We stress more over the things we can't control than we stress over that which we can. As soon as you realize a situation is beyond your control, let loose of it. Letting loose doesn't mean you don't care about the outcome, it means you are liberating yourself from the stress that comes with trying to control things you can't. When these situations occur, say to yourself (out loud if you need to; sometimes it's more helpful): "This is out of my control. There is nothing I can do to control this situation. I'm letting loose of the stress, anxiety and worry caused by not being able to control this situation."

I can't control how people will respond to this book. Like the 4 types of students I mentioned earlier, some will "get around" reading it; some will "get through" reading it; others will "get from" reading it and even some may "give to" reading it. I can only put the information out there. What people do with it is totally out of my control. I accept that and let loose!

The things you need to let loose of are things that are weighing you down and causing you stress and anxiety actually provide little to no value for holding on to them. These listed above are only a handful of suggestions. Can you add to the list? What are some things in your life that would ease your stress level if you simply let loose of it?

Hold on to Hope

Never let loose of hope! There are many things to let loose of in life, but one to never let loose of is hope! There is always hope! As desperate as things appear or as permanent as your struggle may seem, never lose hope. You will find that continuing to move forward, placing one foot in front of the other, will lead to a stronger you and eventually better times.

Reminders and Action Items from Chapter 5

We are all holding onto something(s) that we need to let loose of. Letting loose relieves the weight that we are carrying and lightens our load to be healthier and more productive.

1) Which of the Let Loose items in this chapter can you relate to and why?

2) How has holding onto these Let Loose items impacted you?

3) List some things that you may need to Let Loose of that are not mentioned in the chapter and why.

4) Develop a strategy to Let Loose of the things that are keeping you from reaching your goals.

5) Write down five things you are hopeful about.

Chapter 6

Laugh

Laughter is indeed the best medicine. Nothing makes you feel better than a breathtaking laugh. This may be why great comedians make more money than great doctors! We actually feel better after laughing for an hour straight than sitting in the doctor's office waiting on a diagnosis.

I can remember riding in the backseat of our family car as a kid with my cousin, and she and I would make each other laugh. When we really got going it would get on my mom's nerves and she would say, "stop all that giggling!" We would try to dial it back, but with one simple look at each other, we would explode into laughter. The harder we tried to stop laughing the harder we actually laughed. Mom had to pull the car over on a few long trips so we could catch our breath and so she could calm her nerves.

Though I don't laugh that hard as often, I have definitely maintained my sense of humor. Humor is something I look for in every situation if at all possible. Certain situations are not funny, so I make sure to not go there. Whenever possible, however, I like to get in a good laugh and make others laugh as well.

Recently I took a group of people sky diving. Notice I said, I took a group of people sky diving. I didn't actually sky dive myself. They definitely wanted me to join, but as I have already explained, I have let loose of the pressure people try to put on me! They said I was afraid! I said I had too much to live for! Besides, someone has to be on the ground to call the loved ones in the event things don't go according to plan.

When we arrived at the jump site our group was taken into this room set up like a classroom for the pre-jump meeting. We had 6 divers and 3 non divers in our group, and they let us all go into the meeting. This guy started out walking us through step by step everything that was going to take place from that moment until touching ground. He talked about the gear, the tandem jumper who jumps with you and the landing process. He was an upbeat guy who really got everyone excited and pumped up about skydiving. He looked at me and the other non-divers just before he exited the room and said, "Everyone watch this short video, and I'll be back to sign you three up to jump as well!"

He almost had me convinced! Then he pushed play on the video. I was expecting it to be a video showing people jumping and getting everyone excited about it with a bit of training sprinkled in. NOPE! It was a 6 minute video of a guy who looked like an undertaker talking about all the dangers of sky diving. He talked about the risk involved, and how each diver could potentially die today, and that if you do, you take full responsibility and will not hold them liable. Not what I expected, and that's probably what made me start to laugh. It was such a stark contrast from what I was expecting, and before I knew it I'm shaking from laughing so hard. The divers didn't think the video was funny at all, and that made me laugh even harder! Their mouths were hanging open in horror, and I'm having the best laugh I've had in a while. It was so good! I needed that! I had been anxious about people I care about skydiving, and the laughter alleviated my anxiety. After that laugh, the day was so enjoyable. The weather was nice, and visibility was great. We could see them jump from the plane all the way to the landing. It was the laughter that set the tone and attitude for what could have been an intense day. Laughter makes all the difference.

Now, you have to be careful about gaining comedic value at other people's expense. Some things we laugh at can be hurtful to others and I am not suggesting that it is justified at all. In fact, I am totally against laughing at things that are hurtful to others. However, the skydivers were a pretty close group, and no one was offended by my humor in this situation. When the handler came back in, he asked if I was ready to jump. I got another good laugh in, and then said, "Nah, I'm good!" I had gotten all the entertainment I needed.

The dives went great, and I am actually considering doing it myself at some point. We had such a good time enjoying what was a bucket list day for many in the group. Laughing and being anxiety free made it that much more enjoyable. That is the power of laughter.

Laughter is contagious. It is said that a large percentage of laughter is due to other people laughing, and not so much to the original source of the laughter. Once people get going, it is hard not to join in. Comedy clubs actually hire professional laughers to sit in the audience and laugh at jokes, because they know laughter is contagious. I laugh twice as hard and as often when seeing comedy live as opposed to on screen. It's being in the presence of others laughing that provides the multiplier. My kids had some of their college friends over for game night. They were upstairs playing board games with some pretty bombastic laughers! Once they got started laughing it was so loud and hysterical that we were downstairs laughing, not even knowing the source of their laughter. We said, "You guys have to come back over for game night because we had such a good time!" They probably thought we were crazy because we weren't even a part of the games.

The benefits of laughter are tremendous. Laughter is credited with lowering cortisol levels, the stress hormone in our bodies. Simultaneously, laughter releases endorphins in the body that make us feel good and sometimes even euphoric. It can also be a great workout! When you laugh you bring in oxygen at a much higher rate than normal breathing, and you tighten your abdominal muscles. I've laughed so hard, that it's made my abs sore. That is so much more fun than a trip to the gym. The biggest benefit of developing a healthy sense of humor is its attraction quality. Others want to be around jovial, light-hearted people, and these types commonly attract other people to them.

One of the things that prevents us from laughing is taking ourselves, everyone, and everything too seriously. Seriously! There is a time when we need to be serious, but it's not all of the time. I've been asked on a few occasions to give the eulogy at a funeral. A eulogy is the 5-10 minute portion of the funeral service that honors the person who is deceased. It is an awesome responsibility and can be a very difficult thing to do. Many people have said that they would rather be in the casket than have to deliver the eulogy. I was asked to give the eulogy of a 64 year old man one time and found it very difficult to capture in 10 minutes what it took him 64 years to accomplish. I told a few funny stories about him, and the people in attendance laughed and cried. The laughter had a healing affect during that heavy time. It helped those grieving his death lighten the load of their loss. If we are serious all of the time, then we may miss the tremendous benefits laughter can provide.

People have told me I should be a comedian. Uh no! I'm funny, but I'm not a comedian. I actually tried to write comedy once, and it was not very good. Besides, comedians have too much pressure on them because they have to be funny. As a professional speaker, I don't have to be funny, so, If I do say something that makes people laugh, then it's a bonus. I do have some friends who are comedians, and they get great enjoyment from making others laugh. Often much of the laughter is at their own expense. They tell self-deprecating jokes about themselves and situations they've been in, and they don't take themselves too seriously. The more serious we take ourselves, the more uptight we seem to be.

I encourage you to develop and broaden your sense of humor. You do that by looking for the humor and lighter side of things, anticipating the funny. I've learned that we pretty much find what we look for. If we look for the sad in situations, then sad is what we find. If we look for the humor in situations, then humor is what we find. So be deliberate in your approach to laughter. Remember there is a time and place for everything, and you want to be tasteful and appropriate with humor. Humor at the expense of hurting or embarrassing others isn't worth it, especially if the other person isn't cool with it. Some people are better at dealing with embarrassment, and even welcome it, if it has entertainment value for their friends. This is where you have to use your best judgment.

I was driving by a Walmart once and two shoppers pulled out double heading on a scooter. The one on the very back was using a 12 pack of toilet paper to lean back on for a cushion. It was a funny sight to see for sure. I wanted to capture that moment with a photo for my archives and got caught by them taking the photo. Even though the person on the scooter laughed herself, I still felt bad because it was at their expense.

There are plenty of things to make you laugh in this world. I have gotten some of my best laughter speaking and working with students. Students are hilarious and provide great entertainment value, and for that I say, "THANK YOU!" You too can enjoy the health benefits and stress relief that laughter provides. Make a point to find the funny and anticipate laughter, and you will multiply those moments and feel much better for it.

Reminders and Action Items from Chapter 6

Laughter is the best medicine and it does the body good! It releases endorphins into your body that help you feel better.

1) Find the "funny" in stressful situations

2) Be sure not to laugh at others expense when it may be hurtful.

3) Think about one of the best laughs you ever had and write down the story of it. You will find yourself laughing as you write.

4) What is your favorite joke and tell it to someone to make them laugh.

Conclusion

Stress and anxiety happen to everyone. If I somehow found a way to eliminate it, then I would be one of the wealthiest people in the world. It's a part of life, and we can only hope to manage it effectively. Just C-H-I-L-L-L is my attempt to help you begin to put actionable steps in place to help manage the stress and anxiety in your life. My hope is this book will be a reference for you that you can reach to for years to come. I always thought, and was told, that life gets easier as you go, and that simply isn't true. In fact, life has gotten more challenging as my career and family have grown. I have found, though, that the struggle makes me stronger, and being able to manage the difficult parts of life is very rewarding. Many people wish things to be easier, but that's not realistic. What is realistic and doable is teaching and training yourself to manage difficult, stressful situations. You may not put in to practice the entire C H I L L L, but use the letters that do work and fit within your personality and situation. You may be a H-I-L-L person or an I-L-L person. That's chill for me! You work what's best for you, that's what I'll be doing....CHILLLING!

Works Cited

Sonneberg, Joel. Lewis, Gregg. *Joel*. Harper Collins, 2004. Print.

UC Davis Health Medical Center. *"Gratitude is Good Medicine"* Feature *Nov. 25, 2015*